THE ROMANCE OF MAGNO RUBIO

Lonnie Carter

with Loy Arcenas

*based on the short story
"The Romance of Magno Rubio"
by Carlos Bulosan*

additional dialogue in Filipino by Ralph B Peña

BROADWAY PLAY PUBLISHING INC
224 E 62nd St, NY, NY 10065
www.broadwayplaypub.com
info@broadwayplaypub.com

THE ROMANCE OF MAGNO RUBIO
© Copyright 2011 by Lonnie Carter

First printing: February 2005
Second printing, revised: December 2011
I S B N: 978-0-88145-260-0

Book design: Marie Donovan
Typographic controls & page make-up: Adobe InDesign
Typeface: Palatino
Printed and bound in the U S A

THE ROMANCE OF MAGNO RUBIO was produced
in a workshop production by the Ma-Yi Theater
Company (Jorge Z Ortoll, Executive Director; Ralph
B Peña, Artistic Director) at the Blue Heron Arts
Center, opening on 3 May 2002. The cast and creative
contributors were:

PRUDENCIO... Rolando Garcia III
CLARO... Jojo Gonzalez
ATOY/CLARABELLE..................................Orville Mendoza
MAGNO RUBIO .... Orlando Pabotoy
NICK... Kaipo Schwab

Direction, scenic & costume design................... Loy Arcenas
Lighting design ....James Vermeulen
Movement consultant .... Kristin Jackson
Production stage manager .... Cristina Sison
Rehersal stage manager.. April Kline
Assistant stage managers ....James Gregg & Sacha Reyes

The world premiere of THE ROMANCE OF MAGNO RUBIO was produced by Ma-Yi Theater Company at the D R 2 Theater, opening on 18 October 2002. The cast and creative contributors were:

PRUDENCIO..Ron Domingo
CLARO.. Jojo Gonzalez
ATOY/CLARABELLE.............................Ramon De Ocampo
MAGNO RUBIO... Orlando Pabotoy
NICK...Arthur Acuña

Direction & scenic design .... Loy Arcenas
Costume design .... Myung Hee Cho
Lighting design ....James Vermeulen
Movement consultant .... Kristin Jackson
Sound design..Fabian Obispo
Production stage manager ....April Kline
Assistant stage manager ....Claire Hewitt

CHARACTERS & SETTING

CHORUS, *3-5 men*
MAGNO RUBIO, *the first among equals*
NICK, *our narrator*
CLARO, *in search of El Dorado*
PRUDENCIO, *the cook*
ATOY, *the Instigator*
CLARABELLE

Time: 1930s and beyond

Space: A bunkhouse for migrant farm workers. California.

(Each of our Pinoys enters playing crude instruments, making rhythms, blending together until the last one bangs a discordant note and stops all in their musical tracks. And so, PRUDENCIO begins.)

PRUDENCIO: Sus Maria 'Sef,
You'll make me deaf yet
Let's hear the drop of the pin
And let the games begin *(Rhythms begin anew.)*

CHORUS: Magno Rubio Filipino boy.
Magno Rubio Fili-Pinoy.
Magno Rubio four feet six inches tall.
Magno Rubio dark as a coconut ball.

NICK: We were F O Bs fresh off the boats
When some S O Bs in ties and coats
Said,

ATOY: "Good jobs are yours, wages so fine.
Sign your X's and O's on the dotted line.

CLARO: We love all Filipinos, especially you.

PRUDENCIO:
We treat you with respect and dignity too."

CLARO:
We put down our marks and some signed our names
We got so excited,

ALL: Like kissing new dames

NICK: America the land of honey and cream

MAGNO: We met our new boss,

PRUDENCIO: We were Foreman Peña's team

MAGNO: We jumped in the back of a pickup truck

PRUDENCIO: Filipinos on wheels, now S O L outta luck

CLARO: They showed us our bunk—

ATOY: Stunk funk who'd a-thunk

CLARO: Where recently hens
Had died from disease and shrieked in their pens.

MAGNO: A mattress of metal,

PRUDENCIO: A floor of wood

CLARO: Or concrete

NICK: Or dirt

MAGNO: Was home to our backs,

ALL: Our joints all hurt

CLARO: Up at dawn

NICK: Out in the field

MAGNO: Picking the crop,

PRUDENCIO: Gleaning the yield.

ALL: Neighbor to neighbor in labor called "stoop"

CLARO: Then back after dusk to our chicken coop.

ATOY: Bitter and angry, but not without humor,

NICK: It keeps us all breathing

PRUDENCIO: But one of our kind, amid all the seething

CLARO: Yes, one among us is innocent still

ALL: He's Magno the Rube, he climbs every hill

ATOY: Magno Rubio

ALL: Filipino boy

ATOY: Magno Rubio

ALL: Fili—Pinoy

Magno Rubio four feet six inches tall

Magno Rubio dark as a coconut ball

MAGNO: With a head small

ATOY: And limbs like a turtle

CLARO: A lusty young hare

NICK: And twice as fertile

PRUDENCIO: Now picking peas in the San Jose hills

MAGNO: A quarter an hour

ALL: Don't pay our bills

ATOY: In rain, shine or mudslide he's always stooped

CLARO: *Pagod na pagod, palaging* [tired, he's always] pooped

MAGNO: He's not without hope, *todos los dias* [every day]

ATOY: Fantasia *amor* for all *senoritas*

PRUDENCIO:
One sticks in his brain and drains his *cabeza* [head]
With jugs of wine

ALL: And *fria cerveza* [cold beer]

NICK: He moons and moans at the lovelorn adverts

CLARO: *Tangina!* [Son of a bitch] He's found one

ATOY: From the back page he flirts

MAGNO: In love with a girl he has never seen

PRUDENCIO:
From the Arkansas hills and Little Rock mean

ATOY: A girl twice his size sideward and upward

CLARO: *Binibining panaginip,* [Girl of my dreams]

ATOY: Wideward and cupward

(Then all "whistles" 2 X.)

PRUDENCIO: Magno screws up his fish eyes, they shine like mud

ATOY: They're about to pop out, they're pounding with blood

CLARO: He jumps up so fast like a monkey in heat

NICK: He bites off a chunk of chewing tabac

ATOY: He coughs up a wad and spits on his feet

ALL: Then leaps in the air and rolls on his back

MAGNO: I LOVE HER!

(The NARRATOR/NICK *appears.)*

NARRATOR: It was early spring and the sun outside was glittering on the dew-laden hills, where the royal crowns of edelweiss, the long blue petals of multi-colored poppies were shaking slightly in the wind.
It was morning and we had no work.
Some members of our crew were sleeping in their straw beds, some playing cards in a corner of the bunkhouse, some playing musical instruments on the porch.

(The CHORUS *pounces.)*

ATOY: Hey, Magno, let's play some blackjack
Give you a chance to win your money back
Fill your pockets with dollars, fives, even a ten

CLARO: Then we'll drive into town to Jezebel's den
Atoy will play the mandolin
Nickie will dance—look at him grin!

ATOY: Prudencio's got his shoes polished real slick

PRUDENCIO: Atoy the Peanut oils his *kabayo* [horse-like] dick

CLARO: Prudencio is stirring the pot
We'll drag him along, like it or not

ATOY: The ladies are begging for you, Magno
They want your special brand of touch
They're aching for you, Magno
Muchacha gordita [Fat, juicy lady] wants you extra
mucho much

MAGNO: No more whore
NO MORE WHORE!

CLARO, ATOY & PRUDENCIO: More whore
MORE WHORE!

MAGNO: I am pure of heart—once again
I save myself for my angel
I am good of soul—once again
Magandang [Beautiful] Clarabelle—angel

ATOY: Angel?

CLARO: With a wingspread of a condor

ATOY: Angel?

CLARO: What was that about a tall blonde whore

ATOY: Six feet tall and one ninety-five

PRUDENCIO: Holy Moly, she'll eat him alive

CLARO: I don't care to be there and see him stop
breathing

ATOY: Though I'd like some myself, for her I'd stop
breathing

PRUDENCIO: O no you wouldn't, you've a wife back
home

ATOY: Not seen in three years, a man's got to roam

MAGNO: I like women tall

CHORUS: Don't short men all

MAGNO: I like women big

CHORUS: All small men dig

MAGNO: I like the six feet one ninety-five

PRUDENCIO: *Jesu Kristo*, she'll eat you alive
She'll chew you up fine in small little pieces
You won't know what hit you, your mouse will be
meeses

CLARO: In love with a girl he has never seen
From Arkansas

ATOY & CLARO:Via
A magazine

MAGNO: I LOVE HER!

(NICK *as* NARRATOR *addresses us.*)

NARRATOR: We were pursuing the daily routine of our lives when we had no work. And we were thinking of Magno Rubio's romance with a girl in the mountains of Arkansas. A girl he'd found, with Claro's help, in a lonely heart's magazine.

CLARO: You're out of your gourd! She's twice your size, sideward and upward.

MAGNO: Has size got anything to do with love?

CLARO: That's what I've heard from my uncle.

MAGNO: Your uncle could be wrong.

CLARO: My uncle couldn't be wrong. He was a gentleman. Ask Prudencio.

PRUDENCIO: He is cooking. Do not ask Prudencio when he is cooking.

CLARO: *'Sus, Maria, 'Sef,* what are you cooking now?

PRUDENCIO: Balut under glass/Prairie dog adobo/ *Pinyas* [Pineapples] for dessert/with snot sauce for bobo

CLARO: Oooo, *Manong* [Big brother], watch your snout/I'll yank your nose hairs out

PRUDENCIO: The uncle in question—a gentleman's gent His motto for lent—Keep it limp, keep it bent

From Mardi Gras to Easter
He strapped it to his keester
But forty days later he already went

CLARO: *Supot!* [Uncircumcized!]

PRUDENCIO: They'll catch you up right soon and you'll be sunk
Before you know it, looking out at Alcatraz
And thinking about

ATOY, MAGNO & PRUDENCIO: All that Jazz

CLARO: I have a plan, dear old man

PRUDENCIO: What does it involve, school, college, marriage?

ATOY: Prostitution?

CLARO: *Bakla?* Tomboy?

(MAGNO turns to NICK, our NARRATOR.)

MAGNO: Nick, you go to college? College Boy Nick!

CLARO: College Boy Nickie!

NICK: Now and again I matriculate, Magno.

CLARO: Hey Magno—matriculate—that means he does your mother.
You going to let him get away with that?

NICK: It means I go to school, Magno, when I have enough money.

MAGNO: Like now?

NICK: Like NOT now.
What do you need to know about love, Magno?
I've read all the poems.

MAGNO: O K, what do the poems say?
Has size got anything to do with love?

NICK: "And when I feel, fair creature of an hour
That I shall never look upon thee more

Never have relish in the fairy power
Of unreflecting love, then on the shore
Of the wide world I stand alone and think
'Til love and fame to nothingness do sink."
No, Magno, I don't think size has anything to do with love.

MAGNO: See, Claro, now go away to your El Dorado.

CLARO: This illiterate peasant tells me to go away? I will go to MY El Dorado when I am good and ready to claim my fortune. *Oh di ba* [Isn't that right], Prudencio?

PRUDENCIO: Do not ask Prudencio when he is cooking.

CLARO: From now on I cook for myself.

PRUDENCIO: Hell is other cooks.

CLARO: Cooks and illiterate peasants.

MAGNO: Claro, out of my sight!

CLARO: This ignoramus tells a man who has gone to the second grade "out of my sight"!
Listen, peon—

MAGNO: Here's a dollar. Now go away. Drink the wine in your El Dorado room. I was crazy to pay for it anyway.

CLARO: Look, *Igorot*— *(Racial curse)*

MAGNO: Here's two dollars. Be a gentleman like your uncle.

CLARO: My uncle Tio Pepe was not wrong
God bless his soul, in all the years he spoke
He never gave me bad advice, so long
As I was not the one who said, "Your joke..."
For God bless Tio Pepe, he had one
Joke that he told every time he saw you
One joke about a little dog who runs
Right over to the big dog and says,

CLARO & PRUDENCIO: "Boo!"

CLARO: Now big dog's the watchdog who's been asleep
And little dog's job's to watch big dog snore
And when the burglar sees the sleeping heap

ATOY, CLARO & PRUDENCIO:
It's little dog who saves the day and more

CLARO: And that's my uncle's joke, not once did I
Say, Tio Pepe, why o why o why

MAGNO: What are you saying? You're driving me
crazy!

CLARO: You ask if size has WHAT to do with love?
You hear my Unc? This small dog big dog shove
You think big dog love little dog at all?
That big dog not little dog ball.

MAGNO: What are you talking, you're driving me nuts?
You and your stupid Unc and his dogs' butts
Blow it out your blow-hole, you ugly goat
Throw you and your bunghole in a shithouse boat
Here's FIVE dollars! Be a gentleman's gentleman like
your uncle's uncle

(CHORUS *enchains* CLARO.)

ATOY: See, Claro—money before you
grab that jug of wine
and off to your room
where pleasures await you

PRUDENCIO: Your uncle rests very nice in his grave
The only place he can't misbehave

ATOY: Your uncle's uncle?

PRUDENCIO: Wasn't he the one
so drunk that he fell off a *carabao (Ox-like animal)*
and croaked face down in a pile of *carabao* plop

ATOY: Or was that your uncle's uncle's fish-faced
whoreson's mother's pimpshit cop?!

CLARO: *Igorots* all! *(He storms off to his room, money and wine in hand.)*

PRUDENCIO: Deal from the top of the deck
Or risk your tawny neck

ATOY: This one's shaved just right

PRUDENCIO: Okay, *guapo* [Pretty young man], you've got a fight

MAGNO: I like you to write a letter for me, Nick.

NICK: Where to?

MAGNO: My girl in Arkansas.

NICK: I thought you've been writing to her.

MAGNO: In a way.

NICK: I can't express your feelings, Magno.

MAGNO: Sure you can. I'll dictate in our dialect and you translate it into English.

(We hear in the direction of CLARO'*s room, a bed squeaking like a dozen little pigs.)*

*(*MAGNO *and* NICK *take this in.)*

MAGNO: I have Clarabelle. And Claro has Claro.
You see, he's been writing my letters, but he's very expensive.

NICK: How much did you pay him?

MAGNO: It's very complicated. At first it was only a gallon of wine. Later he thought of making some money. I don't know where he had stolen the idea, but it must have been from the movies. He demanded five dollars per letter.

NICK: That's reasonable, Magno. After all, he spent some money when he went to the second grade.

MAGNO: You see, I wrote my girl every day. I earn only two dollars fifty cents a day. You're our bookkeeper,

Nick. Can you believe those numbers? Still, I had to write to her. I love her. You understand, Nick? That's not the end of it, Nick. Realizing that I truly love the girl, that I can't live in the world without her, he demanded one cent per word.

NICK: One cent per word? It's robbery!

MAGNO: Yes, and he wrote long letters that I couldn't understand. And he used big words. How would I know he wasn't writing for himself?

NICK: It's hard to say.

MAGNO: However, I'm not worried about that part of the deal.
I've confidence in myself.

(Just then MAGNO *swallows a wad of chewing tobacco, grunts and starts to gag.)*

(The CHORUS *is on him like a flash.)*

ATOY: Bite a twist of chunk tobac
Roll it 'round from cheek to cheek

PRUDENCIO: Cough up slime your jaw so slack
Mucus green drips from your beak

ATOY: Lick the brown shreds of saliva
Dripping down your thick lips blue
Bare your ugly mouth more dead than live-a

PRUDENCIO: Your teeth so black

ALL: HOW CAN YOU STAND YOU!

(MAGNO, back from the dead though barely, gasping, wheezing with all his might, declares—

MAGNO: I've confidence in myself!
Claro charged me ten cents per word.
I paid him twenty dollars per letter!
How do I know that what I said he heard
Then put my thoughts as his, making him better

Do you think he's that low, Nick?
Me he would cheat, me he would trick?

NICK: Some men would do anything bad, Magno
Some men would crawl on their bellies on human filth
to earn a dollar.

MAGNO: That's so sad, Nick.
I thought we were all born honest.

NICK: We *were all* born honest. But along the way some
of us lost our honesty.

MAGNO: I didn't lose my honesty.

NICK: They say honesty is the best policy.

MAGNO: That's what I've heard. Still—
Honesty—the best policy
I don't understand, Nick
If I'm an honest person
And Claro next door or next bunk, and he's not so
   honest
How does MY policy of honesty,
do me any good

NICK: You're wrestling with good and evil

MAGNO: I'm wrestling with good and—wait—I don't
WANT to wrestle with evil
Evil's going to win
It's got sin—sin—sin on its side

NICK: Ah, but sin is always on the side
The task—the task—is to keep sin ON its side
And then to turn it over on its back like a turtle
So it can't move, so it's immobilized.

MAGNO: Immobilized?

NICK: So it has no mobility.

MAGNO: Mobility?

NICK: So, it can't get around much—

(With MAGNO*)*

NICK: —anymore.

MAGNO: So it misses the Saturday dance?

NICK: That's right! So it misses the Saturday dance and
it can't make us do what we don't want to do.

MAGNO: Dance how we don't want to dance
But what if I WANT to dance every which way
Like I want to whirl and spin Clarabelle
   and blow all the whistles and ring all the bells
And who's to blame
   for the way I feel
   and should I feel the same as if I'm the one to blame
Nick, Nick, please help me now
Holy Carabao, Holy Cow
I'm free, tell me I'm free because I've got you
Will you write for me, Nick? Clarabelle and I thank
   you.

NICK: I couldn't have put it better, Magno. Sure, you
   bet, of course
I'll write for you
What more can I ask than to do this task
Not a "task", but a pleasure to see this through

MAGNO: What would you like to have?

NICK: Have? Have?
I have everything I need.

MAGNO: How can you? You don't drink a drop of wine

NICK: Not so, but only if it's very fine.

MAGNO:
You never chase the girls, 'though they like you.

NICK: I like them too; it's just I'm never through.

MAGNO:
Through what? There's always time for women where
The women wear whatever they do wear

And it drives me crazy in these magazines
The way they look, so ready in these scenes
Kabayos [Horses] and *kambings* [goats] ready to mount
All of them beauties too many to count
And you, you want none of it, why is that?
You don't gamble and you don't smoke cigars
You don't even chew, just gaze at the stars

NICK: The stars, dear Magno, are where poets go

MAGNO: That's where I want to go, Nick.

NICK: We'll get you there, *kaibigan* [friend, compatriot].

MAGNO: *Kaibigan.*
That's what I like about you, Nick. You use your
college education in the right direction.

NICK: I'll write for you because I like to help you.
Maybe I'll need your help someday.
By the way, how do you know your girl in Arkansas is
so tall and big?

MAGNO: She wrote to me.

NICK: You mean Claro told you what she wrote.

MAGNO: Exactly.

NICK: Did she send you a picture of herself?

MAGNO: This is it.

(MAGNO *pulls out wads of paper, magazine clippings
from "men's" mags, and finally hands* NICK *a crumpled
snapshot.*)

(NICK *examines it, clearly not being able to make much of
it.*)

NICK: How tall is she according to Claro?

MAGNO: Six feet tall in bare feet

(*The* CHORUS *pounces.*)

ATOY & PRUDENCIO: She'll eat him alive, he's raw meat

MAGNO: I like women tall

ATOY & PRUDENCIO: Don't short men all?

MAGNO: I like women big

ATOY & PRUDENCIO: All small men dig

MAGNO: One ninety-five of pure weight

ATOY: Jesus Cristo, he can't wait
She'll swallow him whole
devour him clean

PRUDENCIO: Jack Sprat AND his wife
eating fat and lean

MAGNO: I will court her as no man has ever courted
before.

(CLARO *bursts out of his room.*)

CLARO: You can't court this lady from ArkanSAWS
White and tight and strawberry blonde to boot
She's squeaky clean, you're mud-caked from jaw to
  paws
You never wash your clothes, you ain't got no suit

MAGNO: I do I do yes I do wash my clothes
And yes I do have a suit of fine thread

CLARO: Shreds of rags brown as your coconut head
You stink up the bunkhouse, I hold my nose
And race out for fresh air when you sit to eat
Companion of pigs and rotten goat meat

MAGNO:
I'll show you, Claro, who's clean and who's not
I'll throw all my rags in a pot too hot
Then I'll put on my suit and strut my stuff
I'm Magno Rubio tougher than tough

ALL: He's Magno Rubio tougher than tough

ATOY: He'll put on his suit and strut his stuff

PRUDENCIO: He'll throw all his rags in a pot too hot

ATOY:
He'll show you, Claro, who's clean and who's not

CLARO: Go rip off your rags and steam them a lot
And please please burn them in fire so hot
And blow off the smoke ten miles from shore,
Where sharks and tuna and whales galore
Can shut down their gills and hold their spouts
You're a skunk with the shits—now—keep—your—
stink—out!

MAGNO: I 'm doing it doing it burning the lot
Then I'm taking a bath in the hottest of pots
I'll be clean and squeaky, ready for her
Her Arkansas Sass, her blondest of fur

CLARO: Don't take off your rags, we'll all have to leave
The rats in the outhouse will upchuck and heave

MAGNO: Here goes here goes you asked, you shit
This skunk with the shits is giving you it

NARRATOR/NICK: We dashed out of the house to the
foothills for fresh air.
But even then our stomachs betrayed us and made us
curse the ugliness of some human beings.
However, it was over. Magno Rubio was a human
being again. He had Clarabelle. He was in love for the
first time in his life.

(CLARABELLE's *voice*, CLARABELLE's *presence*.)

CLARABELLE: Magno, such a big name and so so strong
I long to be with you and hold you tight
When first love comes, to both of us belong
the rites of spring; the world's room all night
will show us how we touch each other's soul
The world's room so soft and warm, invites
our arms and legs to intertwine and roll
each other up in whiteout sand and nights
of gritty bliss; we'll kiss our rearing heads

and scale the mountains, plumb the river pools
sniff the forests, lie upon their beds
of leaves and moss, and trace each others jewels
Smoke our makanudos like fools
Polish our *makamundo* [earthy] tools
Break all the *El dorado* rules
Como Todos los Santos [Like all saintly spirits] ghouls
And join each other—*bulbul* [pubic har] to *bulbul*
Makanudo makamundo lalo [more cigar, more earthy]
Makanudo makamundo lalo

(MAGNO *has swooned but now regains himself.*)

MAGNO: Will you write a letter now, Nick? And maybe use some of those poem words?

NICK: Sure, Magno. How about— "Why so pale and wan, fond lover..."

MAGNO: That sounds good, Nick, real mysterious, like I don't know what it means, but it's pretty, like Clarabelle. (*He immediately scrambles to get a pencil and pad of notepaper and a huge dictionary.*)

NICK: We don't need the dictionary.

MAGNO: *Marami lalo salita malaki*

NICK: I thought you didn't want a lot of big words.

MAGNO: *Mas maganda kung mas maraming salitang malalim* [It's more beautiful if it has bigger, deeper words] (*He says "Ikaw" three times, because no other words come to him.*)

(*Finally some words struggle forth with* NICK'S *assistance [last verse from the song].* NICK *translates as* MAGNO *speaks.*)

MAGNO:	NICK:
Ikaw ang ligaya sa buhay	You are the joy in life

Sa piling mo'y walang
    kamatayan
	In you're arms
	    there is no death

Puso ko'y nangumpisal	My heart confesses
Sa birheng dalanginan	To the Blessed Virgin
Na ang pangarap ko'y *ikaw*	That you are my dream

(The song Ikaw develops from the letter. As NICK *writes,* MAGNO *"dances" with* CLARABELLE.*)*

Ikaw [You] *(By Mike Velarde)*

Ikaw ang aking panaginip [You are my dream]
Ikaw ang tibok ng dibdib [The beating of my heart]
Pusong umiibig [A heart that loves]
Dinggi't umaawit [Listen to it sing]
Tinataghoy ay pag-ibig. [Longing for true love]

Ikaw ang ligaya sa buhay [You are the joy in life]
Sa piling mo'y walang kamatayan [In your arms there is no death]
Puso ko'y nangumpisal [My heart confesses]
Sa birheng dalanginan [To the blessed Virgin]
Na ang pangarap ko'y ikaw [That you are my dream]

Ikaw ang ligaya sa buhay
Sa piliong mo'y walang kamatayan
Puso ko'y nangumpisal
Sa birheng dalanginan
Na ang pangarap ko'y ikaw

(When the song ends, NICK *addresses us again.)*

NICK: It was the middle of spring and we were picking peas on the hillside near our bunkhouse. Magno Rubio and I were working side by side, astride neighboring rows that began from the slope of the hills and ended atop a stony plateau.

ATOY: Prudencio, on Foreman Peña
Let's play a trick, pretend to be sick

PRUDENCIO: Atoy the instigator, watch your back
Before you get us all tied in a sack

ATOY: Where is your sense of derring-do, so tough?

PRUDENCIO: The scars across my neck are quite enough

NICK: Foreman Peña?
He was the best of the worst

(It's CHORUS *time: 7 single counts of stick work then thunder clap on the 7ᵗʰ count)*

NICK: Suddenly black clouds descended and a storm
   opened upon us
And still we held our ground
It's pouring rain and we're picking grapes, catching rye

CLARO:
It's quota time—foreman's standing there so proud
In pancho, repelling the hail, now burst
Upon us drenched, soaked to the skin, fetal
Position, trying any move—

ATOY & CLARO: Keep dry!

PRUDENCIO: Somehow, we must keep dry
We shout we shout!
Make music, holler, chant—

ATOY, CLARO & PRUDENCIO: Hey, Peñaman!

CLARO: What's with you, down and dirty, join us now
We have to make our quota if we can
And you, dear foreman, genuflect and bow
The hail, the rain, our bones about to crack

PRUDENCIO: So help us now, we always got your back
O, just this once, please stoop and help us out

ATOY: Forget you're better, 'cause you're not about
To win this bout, we will prevail and rout
You if this rain ever stops
We'll bust you bust you bust your chops
(He is stuck to the ground.)
Thanks, Mister Foreman Man
Sure is a pleasure to serve you and The Man

MAGNO: And your brown nose as brown as mine,

NICK, MAGNO & PRUDENCIO:
But mine's brown without licking,

CLARO: You eat! Mister Rock Rock

PRUDENCIO: Now get down and get picking!

(Stick work resumes: 8 single/8 double time/12 fast)

NICK: And just as suddenly the storm was over
The foreman, showing us the steep and thorny way to
    heaven
Went back to standing
That early summer smell that filled our heads
With lilacs and primrose and air so clear
We almost thought to wonder without fear

ATOY: When I left the lush of mountain air, I'd barely
    been alive
And now I'm fast approaching an ancient twenty-five
These butterflies, Prudencio,
Their beauty is so light and slow
It almost makes me think that it was right for me to go
Magno, Magno, *tingnan mo—paru-paru* [look, a
butterfly]

NICK: Psst! What are your plans for Clarabelle?

MAGNO: I want to marry her, Nick.

NICK: Would you like to say that in your next letter?

MAGNO: That's what I've been planning to tell you.

NICK: Well, you should propose to her.
How much money have you already spent on her?

(MAGNO starts counting to one hundred by ones.)

NICK: Magno, Magno, a round number.

MAGNO: The engagement ring, seventy-five dollars.
The wrist-watch? Eighty dollars. A pair of suede shoes,

some clothes, a diamond bracelet. Over three hundred dollars!

NICK: That's plenty of money, Magno.

MAGNO: It's worth it, Nick. I'll just have to work harder.

NICK: Harder?

MAGNO: For every pod of pea I pick
one mill is what I earn
For every little mill I get
one word is what I buy
For twenty ears of corn I shuck
one cent is what I put away
For fifty heads of lettuce plucked
two cents will buy— "With love I burn!"
For every bunch of cherries snapped
"I miss you"s what I sigh
One hundred stalks of 'sparagus
for "Love you love love you, love"
I work the livelong day

ATOY, CLARO & PRUDENCIO: Words words words,

CLARO: Now here's the matter,
monkey boy in heat

ATOY, CLARO & PRUDENCIO: Words words words,

ATOY: More veg-e-tables,
Rubio, more fruit

ATOY, CLARO & PRUDENCIO: Fruit fruit fruit,

PRUDENCIO: The bigger harvest
sooner you two meet

ATOY, CLARO & PRUDENCIO: Toe-may-toes,

CLARO: Now here's the matter
tell her she's your beaut

ATOY, CLARO & PRUDENCIO: Words words words,

ATOY: Your knife is steady
go into your crouch

ATOY, CLARO & PRUDENCIO: Fruit fruit fruit,

PRUDENCIO: The crop is ready
see her lounging on her couch

ATOY, CLARO & PRUDENCIO: Work words work,

CLARO: She loves your chatter,
monkey boy in heat

ATOY, CLARO & PRUDENCIO: Words work words,

ATOY: She needs you at her,
wants you to repeat

MAGNO: For every pod of pea I pick
one mill is what I earn
For every little mill I get
one word is what I buy
For twenty ears of corn I shuck
one cent is what I put away
For fifty heads of lettuce plucked
two cents will buy— "With love I burn"
For every bunch of cherries snapped
"I miss you" 's what I sigh
One hundred stalks of 'sparagus
for "Love you love you love you, love"
I work the livelong day
I'm sure I'm sure I never guess
I work for words, these words my work
It's worth it worth it worth it—
YES!

NICK: Suppose she'll change her mind when she
arrives in California?

(The CHORUS imposes itself.)

ATOY: Is there a flicker of momentary doubt
in your little monkey face?

PRUDENCIO: Is that your ticker in its tickytocky shout crying to slow down the pace?

MAGNO: I don't think Clarabelle will do that. She is a good girl.

CLARO: *Ligaw dingin kantot hangin* [Courting a worthless girl]

NICK: I hope you're right.

MAGNO: I've confidence in her.

(NICK/NARRATOR *speaks to the audience.*)

NICK: So two years after Magno's first contact with this phantasm, this chimera, this unattainable giant of our roaring imaginations
I write the letter of proposal and,
lo and behold, she answers immediately.

(CLARABELLE *is heard; her presence is felt.*)

CLARABELLE: I accept your sweet proposal
it's so thrilling reading through it
I accept your sweet proposal
and I'm willing now to do it
Now there are just some small details
I really must attend to
Salvation Army lines too long
The bells they ring drive me ding dong
My family you might lend to
My mom you see is not so well
she's getting up in years
I fear that she won't last 'til Spring
she's causing me such tears
If only I could stay here now
it sure would help me out
Of course, it takes some cash to treat her
and her painful gout
My little sisters brothers, six,
all them are under ten

They're just the nicest cutest things
the youngest is named Ben
Poor Ben he has this problem now
it's all about his school
His classmates made such fun of him
he drowned them in their pool
How he's in the slammer tight
he got into a hammer fight
I'm so afraid he won't last
he has to pay protection fast
Tomorrow tomorrow
tomorrow please Western Union me
My daddy most of all is pleased
and anxious for us two
To be so joined in Holy Mat—
rimony, that's the glue
That sticks me to you you to me
until death do us part
In meantime Daddy has such bills
they mangled up his heart
Tomorrow tomorrow
tomorrow please Western Union me
Back to your sweet proposal, dear,
I have it with me now
My heart is with you now and then
I'm there A S A P
So, darling, handsome Magno love
express your dough to me
Tomorrow tomorrow
tomorrow you Western Union me

MAGNO: Poor girl. She needs more money. Her little sisters and brothers,
all under ten, need more gatas,
more *bakas* [cows], more *gintos* [gold]
more *utongs* [teats]
I'll work like *carabao* and live like *aso* [dog]

The pea season's over
Let the celery the carrots
Begin—
Goo-lay
Goo-lay
Goo-goo
Lay-Lay
Magno kang puti-kan
Sa Ingless ay Muddy Man
Baon sa lupa,
'Nak ng tupa
sahod mo'y lantang lechuga
Sige na
Sige pa
Do nat stop
Magno ka
Isa, dalawa, tatlong kaban na'sparagus lang ang laman
Apat, lima, anim, pito, da bro-koli is pang-walo
Se-ga-dilyas, mustasa, and stawberry's *labing-lima*
Sapol da apple, *one pahabol*
Timabang, kulan, dat is the tro-bol.
Goo-lay, Goo-lay
Goo-goo kang matibay
Pitas-pitas da prutas working-working like a *Hudas*
Todo-todo, parang toro do nat stop 'till *inodoro*
Sige na
Sige pa
Masuwerte na ang may tinga.
Tatlo, Lima, Pitlong taong nagpatong-patong na talong
Sinlaki ng sinkamas,pag-ibig kong tumitigas
Kas-Kas Kas-Kas
Kamay lamang ang pang-lunas
Pas-Pas-Pas-Pas
You make *pas-ter da pag-pitas*

One *Sibuyas,* Two *Lechugas*
Four *'gadilyas,* Six *manasas*

Three *mustasa*, eight *patata*
After dat, *'sa pang pasada*

Two *Kamatis*, Plus da *bawang*
Add da *sitaw*, still it's *kulang*
Pick the *upo*, dig the *gabi*
Di pa kasang, pamasahe
Paulit-ulit, 'til *masulit*

Habol ko ay sampung guhit

MAGNO & CHORUS:
Sige na
Sige pa
Do not stop
Magno ka
One *Sibuyas*, Two *Lechugas*
Four *'gadilyas*, Six *manasas*
Three *mustasa*, eight *patata*
Sige lang ang pag-ratsada
Sige lang ang kalabasa
Sige pa, some more *mustasa*
Sige na, 'sa pang pasada
Sugod gid, por your *pag-asa*
Sulong man, por your *dalaga*
Sige lang ang pag-ratsada
Sige lang ang kalabasa
Sige pa, more *mustasa*
Sugod gid, por your *pag-asa*
Sulong man, *por* your *dalaga*

(*Improvised rhythm and vocalizations start with* CHORUS/
NICK *while* MAGNO *continues his stylized "picking and
cutting".*)

MAGNO: Clarabelle!

CLARABELLE: Will you wait?

MAGNO: I'll wait!

NICK: What quality of soul sustains a man
To have such faith in someone he's not seen
What possibly can he be thinking? Can
He hold such hope when all about him mean
To tell and do tell him he's lost his mind?
When he, beyond all reason and belief
Who should have given up, as others find
No solace in anything, no relief
Except who touches them and whom they touch;
Is this untouchable, this wretched ram
Whose only good would seem to be so much
Of picking, stacking, carting—Jesus damn!
Or does he, Magno Rube, know more than we
And should we turn ourselves so loose—and free

MAGNO: I'll WAIT!

(NICK as NARRATOR addresses the audience.)

NICK: Another season goes by, and then another
We follow the fruits, and the vegetables follow us

PRUDENCIO: from San Jose to Salinas

ATOY: from Napa to Modesto

MAGNO: from grapes to plums

CLARO: from artichokes to cauliflower

PRUDENCIO:
from Washington potatoes and Idaho apples

NICK: or is it the other way 'round
the ends pushing against our middles
and always we come back to this bunkhouse

PRUDENCIO: the tomatoes here are almost frozen with
winter setting in

ATOY: Back in the Philippines,

ALL: Pilipinas,

ATOY: Nothing would have frozen.
Prudencio gets regular letters from Luzon island
He reads them aloud and we are nostalgic—

NICK: We have that pain from our past and for our past

MAGNO:
A salmon arrives in the mail with no return address
the postmark is Juneau

CLARO: And we know that Toto is working the
canneries

NICK: And the next month, or the next

PRUDENCIO: Turing will send us something else

MAGNO: from wherever he is

CLARO: wherever they are
The poker players are shy a few hands
until a new batch of hands arrives, fresh with almost-
hope

NICK: Here it is, holiday time and we have nothing to
do

(MAGNO *decides to oil his hair.*)

CLARO: Magno Rubio is oiling his hair

ALL: Hooray hooray!
Mabuhay Mabuhay!
Long live us all

ATOY: Magno Rubio is oiling his hair

CLARO: He's no doubt going to the finest grand ball

PRUDENCIO: He'll be wined, he'll be dined
he'll dance with fine ladies

ATOY: He'll jump in the air
And shake out his locks
One strand at a time he greases with care
He never minds a nit or two

what's a louse between friends
Or a flea or a gnat,

CLARO: What's that?

ATOY: It's all the same, when love never ends

MAGNO: My Clarabelle will know I'm clean tonight
I'm clean, my soul is clean; my hair is bright
My heart is light; my conscience right

ALL: O, what a sight!

NICK: My pants are tight!

ALL: I have to bite!

MAGNO: Go fly a kite
With all my might
I'll raise my height
And you I'll smite!

ATOY: Smite?

MAGNO: Smote, smitten!

PRUDENCIO: You've been reading the dictionary.

MAGNO: I can't read!

ATOY: You've been sleeping with it under your pillow.

MAGNO: I can't sleep—the words are rushing 'round
my ears
I don't understand
Hindi ko po naiintindihan
Nick, help me, don't stop writing my letters!

NICK: O K, Magno, O K.

MAGNO: I had a nightmare that you'd stopped. Then
what would my Clarabelle think?

NICK: Alright, I'll write more, Magno. For Christmas.

What are you giving Clarabelle for Christmas, Magno?

MAGNO: I'm giving her a radio. A combination radio-
phonograph. It costs me nearly two hundred dollars.

(CLARO *bangs on the table with both fists and leaps to his feet.*)

MAGNO: Listen, you peon, what are you laughing at? I got Clarabelle.

CLARO: Clarabelle, my eye. You mean to tell me that a girl like Clarabelle loves a donkey like you?

MAGNO: What's wrong with me?

CLARO: What's wrong with me?

Don't you know, peasant?

MAGNO: You are also a peasant.

CLARO: An educated peasant!

PRUDENCIO: Second Grade!

CLARO: There, monkey-faced dog-peasant!

MAGNO: I don't care what you say, Clarabelle loves me.

CLARO: Prove it, dog-eater!

(MAGNO *produces an autographed photo from his wallet.*)

MAGNO: Here's the absolute proof.

(CHORUS *adlib: "Ipakita mo sa kanila"; "Picture"; "Dear Magno, 'I love you', Clarabelle"*)

CLARO: You think you are the only man with an autographed photograph from Clarabelle? (*He produces an autographed photo from his wallet.*)

MAGNO: That doesn't prove anything, but this proves something definite. (*He produces a lock of hair.*)

(*Chorus adlib: "Goldilocks"; "Bango"; "Sarap"*)

MAGNO: From her own head.

CLARO: Proof, my ass. This is the irrefutable proof. Look for yourself, pig. (*He puts produces another lock of hair.*)

(*Chorus adlib: "Blonde"; "Kulot"; "Baho"*)

CLARO: And it's not from her head either.

(The CHORUS *ever-present.)*

ALL: Magno Rubio's coconut head sinks into his turtle body.

ATOY: His fish-eyes shine.

PRUDENCIO: His flat black nose flares.

NICK: His ugly mouth snarls.

ALL: His gorilla legs leap!

(Suddenly MAGNO *and* CLARO *are in a furious fight.)*

*(*NICK *and the others break it up.* CLARO, *restrained, still bursts out.)*

*(*MAGNO *is alone and weeping.* PRUDENCIO *comes upon him.)*

PRUDENCIO: Why are you weeping, little one?
Why is your face broken?
How long have you been at this?
This life which makes us all old without cease
What is it when we have no work?
What is it even when we do?
Weep for that that keeps us here
Playing games of cards, so ripped and bent,
my back so stripped and bent
with four or five *manongs* like me
And always one off to the side
with his solitaire
Or strumming battered guitars with broken strings
The wattles of my rooster neck shaking with anger
like a dog with an old shoe in his stinking mouth
Why are you weeping, little one?
Why is your face broken?
How long have you been at this
This life that makes us old without release
What is it when we have no work

What is it even when we do
Weep for coming here across the waters
When we had hope that this land
Would open its arms
And yes it has—open—now shut around us
Parang sawat (Snake indigenous to the Philippines)
The United Snakes of America
Little one, go ahead and weep

ATOY, CLARO, NICK & PRUDENCIO:
Magno Rubio, Filipino boy
Magno Rubio, Fili—Pinoy
Magno Rubio, four feet six inches tall
Magno Rubio, dark as a coconut ball

NICK/NARRATOR: We were packing lettuce in the shade. It was May again and the crop was good. It was now three years and four months since he had first written to her.

NICK: Have you heard from Clarabelle, Magno?

MAGNO: O-o. *Hindi po. Ayokon.* [Yes. No.}
It's no use, Nick. Claro fouled up everything.

NICK: Let's see it.

(MAGNO *hands him a letter.*
And then another
And then another
And then another
Ten in all.)

NICK: Ten letters she wrote and you didn't tell me?

MAGNO: I was afraid.

NICK: Don't be afraid, Magno. Let's see this through.

(NICK *begins to read the letters and we hear* CLARABELLE'S *voice.)*

CLARABELLE:
Magno Rubio, Ruby for short

El Chico
How tall are you when you stand on your Jacksons?
 Just kidding
Magno Ruby, you from the isle of Puerto Rico?
My San Juan Juan, you got a pencil-thin mustache,
that's the action.
JUST KIDDING!
What kind of name is Rubio? Not that I'm Pre—Jew—
Diced, you see
I believe in equal rights for you and especially me
Now you say you want to marry me, cherish and hold
But if I may be so bold—
The last time you wrote you said you'd send me
    cimollions
A hundred or so, I got a sweet tooth, my sweet, for
Napoleons
Die—rect from France.
Not a chance.
I'm kidding!
You got to take me who I am, I'm such a joker
But where's the bread?
El pan and don't spare *la mantequilla*
I know some Spanyole, learned it playin' poker
With an *hombre* from Colombia, lookin' to fill my
    tortilla
But of course I wouldn't let him, I'm savin' myself for
    you
Now how's about those gold dubloons and a piece of
    eight or two
You're my very own pirate with one eye and wooden
    leg
Magno Rubio Ruby, please don't make me beg
Don't you want my long legs wrapped around your
    gaucho?
My golden tresses streaming across your thighs
My orange melons bobbing above your eyes
I'll crack your back and twist your *cojones* [balls]

        —Ole Oucho
So send the bread and the butter too
I'm your *cordero y cerdo* [lamb and sow] —now Chew!

CHORUS: She's your *cordero y cerdo*
—now CHEW!

NICK: I don't know, Magno, it doesn't sound right
The way she talks, she sounds like she's not nice
It's time to tell her where you're from.

MAGNO: Where I'm from?

NICK: She thinks you're from the Southern Hemisphere
She thinks that means it's anywhere but here
You have to tell her first where you're NOT from
And then perhaps perhaps she'll finally come

(Song: You're Not From...*)*

CHORUS: You're not from—
Trinidad Tobago El San y Salvador
Saint Lucia las Malvinas Quito Ecuador
Saint Vincent, Martinique Bolivia and Paraguay
Colombia Puerto Rico y Venezway
(Depeated: "Ay ya ya ya ya")
Panama y Nicaragua Dutch Guyana Surinayme
Costa Rica Argentina Puerto Rico Mehico aren't
all—the—same
Guatemala Hee—Span—Yola
Cuba Chile all say "Hola"
Port au Prince Tonton Macouting
Montserrat volcanoes spewing
King's Jamaica limbo-doing
Saint Martin is looting shooting
*(Repeat "Ay ya ya ya ya" to ...Puerto Rico Mehico aren't
all–the same")*
Pero Clarabelle e blanca [But Clarabelle is white]
no morada, no castana, no morena y no negra [not any
shade of brown or black] *Clarabelle*

MAGNO: She's white, she's blonde, she's like the sun
I'm right, I'm right, she is the one

ATOY: And now, Magno Rubio, you must tell this Like-
the-Sun where
where
where you are from

(Pilipino, Ako Po'y Pilipino)

*(Song of the Philippines. In Tagalog with simultaneous
"translation".)*

MAGNO: *Sa May Bandang Silangan*
Hindi lamang sa kung-saan
And lupang pinanggalingan
Ni Magnong Putikan
Bagama't siya'y isang hamak
Bulsa'y butas at magaan
Sa pag-ibig at romansa'y
Langit lang ang hangganan.
Pagkat wala nang hihigit
Kanino man sa Pilipino
Maging si Romeo-yo man,
O sabihin nang si Balentino.
Matamis siyang magmahal
Puwedeng nang pang-almusal.
Pag-sapit ng gabi'y
Putok niya'y sinlakas
Ng Myon at Taal.
Pilipino.
Ako po'y Pilipino.
Puso'y titibok-tibok
Sa paghihintay, ng iyong alok.
Ay, Clara, giliw ko.
Ito ay para sa 'yo.
Buksan and pinto mo
Sa Pilipinong pipino ko.

(CHORUS enters and sings as MAGNO translates with NICK's help.)

CHORUS:	MAGNO:
Pilipino.	Filipino.
Ako po'y Pilipino.	I am Filipino.
Puso'y titibok-tibok	My heart beats
Sa paghihintay, ng iyong alok.	Waiting for your invitation.
Ay, Clara, giliw ko.	Oh, Clara, my darling.
Ito ay para sa 'yo.	All of this is yours.
Buksan ang pinto mo	*(Open your window,)*
Sa Pilipinong pipino ko.	*(To my Filipino cucumber.)*

(Men cross the stage drunk. Dance with chairs)

CHORUS:
Pilipino, malambing, ma-carino
Sa umaga ang kayod
Gabi nama'y nalilinkod
Ay, blondie, darling *ko*
Pa-tikim naman sa 'yo.
Kung ikaw ay mangga
Ako naman ang iyong tubo.

(Translation of Pilipino song)

There. In the East. There!
No, no. Not just any Where.
But a berth that's baked and bare
Lies, Magno, The Muddy Man's lair.

Though he's as poor as dirt,
His pockets, holey and light.
You'll excuse his plight,
When he loves you, loves you tonight

Ain't no out-doing
The Filipino's wooing
Even if you've Romeo's, Valentino's, or
Or that chap Chaplin's cooing.

The Fili-Pinoy is sweet,
He's good enough to eat.
By day, he works like a tornado,
At night, he'll rumble like a volcano.

(ATOY *sings* Home of the Range)

(*Before they all pass out,* PRUDENCIO *has the last word.*)

PRUDENCIO: Consuelo –
So when do I get to touch you again?
Come now, Prudencio needs you in the night
La Dorada, golden, perfect, you again
I want you, want you, want the light
You smell, you smell, like perfect baby feet
You're home, you're home, I want you even more
I want to be there, at home on the street
Consuelo, la Dorada, I am for
You every moment, I want to come back
I can't get there now, I still owe so much
I work, I cook, I load sacks on my back
I can't get there now, I still owe so much
Dorada, bounce like a ball, to the beat
You love, you smell like perfect baby feet.

(*It's night. The snores, wheezes, grunts, groanings,
eructations and the general nocturnal pandemonial
cacophony of exhausted men at their fitful rest.*)

(CLARO, *however, is not asleep. He's stuffing things from
various spots, things perhaps not his own, into a duffel bag.*)

(NICK, *too, is not asleep and stops* CLARO *as he's about to
leave.*)

NICK: Where to, *manong*?

CLARO: None of your business.

NICK: Only a thief in the night—

CLARO: I'm not stealing anything. My uncle—

NICK: Your uncle? I wouldn't press it.

Where to, *manong*? El Dorado?

CLARO: El Dorado!

NICK:
I'll come with you. I've always wondered where it is.
Prudencio thinks it doesn't exist, but I'm willing to be
persuaded otherwise.

CLARO: I KNOW!

NICK: I'm sure you do.

CLARO: You'd come with me?

NICK: Maybe tomorrow.

CLARO: Ah, Nick, you'll never get anywhere.

NICK: Probably.

CLARO: Move, got to move, no flies on Claro,
Prudencio doesn't get it
Prudencio only
Hit the road, Nick!

NICK: "There's gold in them thar hills, pahdnah."

CLARO:
You think, you read, you think that's something?
Motion—loco—motion!

NICK: *Loco—baliw, ulol, sira*—crazy, broken Claro.

CLARO: You call me crazy, I'll cut out your heart.

NICK: Quiet, Claro, you'll wake everyone and then
you'll have to explain why this bag is so stuffed.

CLARO: I'll leave without you. Keep this stinking stuff.
(He dumps out the stuff.) Stay here—rot—don't move—
(He starts to leave.)

NICK: Claro—

(CLARO stops.)

(NICK goes to him and they embrace.)

(CLARO *leaves.*)

(*It's morning.*)

(NICK's *making notes.*)

(MAGNO *stirs.*)

MAGNO: Hey, college boy, what you are you doing, Nick?

NICK: Reading, Magno.

MAGNO: What are you reading, one of your poems?

NICK: A poem, yes.

MAGNO: Somebody wrote it?

NICK: Somebody wrote it.

MAGNO: I won't understand it.

NICK: Yes, you will. You'll understand enough.

MAGNO: So, read it.

(NICK *reads.*)

NICK: The day is like a trembling heart. Alone
in the harbor, I feel the world burst
in the wide canyons of my thoughts...
I am glad I have seen everything
For there will be days when we will stand together
Fighting for our right to stand together,
I think they will understand why we should
Stand together in our time.

MAGNO: *Napakaganda!* [Very beautiful!]

NICK: Did you understand it enough?

MAGNO: *Kaunti—sapat—o-o.* [Enough, yes]

NICK: *O-o, kaibigan.*

(*The* CHORUS *seizes the moment.*)

ATOY: How long could he wait?

PRUDENCIO:—forever it seems
Because she really wasn't real at all
He—we—we all created her
Beautificated her
from a page in a glossy, saucy, bossy rag
But he was about to pay the piper

ATOY: Cleopatra put the asp to her breast
and Magno would now clasp the viper
Clarabelle would put the snake to his chest
and she would now shove and tie his head in a bag

(End of beat)

(New beat)

(NICK. MAGNO)

NICK: *(Waving a letter)* Magno! She's coming! Clarabelle is on the way!

MAGNO: Did she say she's coming to marry me?

NICK: That's what she says, Magno. Did you save enough money for this emergency?

MAGNO: I've fifty dollars.

NICK: That's not enough.

MAGNO: But I thought—

NICK: You can't marry here, Magno. You can't marry in the whole state of California. And you'll need at least two hundred dollars for the whole affair.

MAGNO: I didn't know it would cost that much to get married.

NICK: It's only the beginning.

MAGNO: Nick, can you loan me some?

NICK: Magno, I can't.

MAGNO: I understand. I'll ask the foreman.

NICK: Again you'll ask.

Magno, you make how much a day, a week, a month?

MAGNO: Year. Years!
Maybe Claro.

NICK: It's worth it to ask Claro?

MAGNO: Do you think she wrote to Claro?

NICK: I don't know.

MAGNO: I will kill him!

NICK: Alaska.

MAGNO: Alaska?

NICK: He left last night—he's prospecting for gold
Or tuna maybe, he's not satisfied
To stay with us, or else he knows it's old
Hat, what we're waiting for, cut and dried
He thinks he'll strike it rich and hit a vein
It's fool's gold in his pan of albacore
We're rootless migrants, lost as Abel's Cain
Who's killed his brother, knowing not what for
It's cauliflower keeps us all oppressed
We push ourselves, gyrating o'er the land
Careering through the groves where olive's pressed
To canneries for smelting packed by hand
The world's our oyster NOT when we're sardines
There's nothing gold about this hill of beans

MAGNO: Nick, what are you saying?
You seem so—so...

NICK: So, what, Magno?

MAGNO: You must be happy.

NICK: Must be? Happy? Yes, Magno, I must be happy.
For you, I'm happy. Suddenly happy.

MAGNO: O good, Nick, you are my light, my dawn
Liwanag—bukang—liwayway
Bukang—liwayway

NICK: And Clarabelle?

MAGNO: She too, Nick. You two—she too.
Bukang—liwayway.

(End scene)

(NICK as NARRATOR speaks to the audience.)

NICK: We were loading crates of lettuce when
a telegram came for Magno Rubio. It was from
Clarabelle. She was arriving in town sooner than she
had expected. He had only four hours to prepare and
we had five more trucks to load. He was stunned for
a moment. Then he started throwing the loaded crates
into the truck, working like two men.
We rushed to the bunkhouse, showered, borrowed
the pickup from the foreman and raced into town. I
saw her immediately. She was the woman in Claro's
snapshot.
Clarabelle?

CLARABELLE: Yes. Are you Claro?

NICK: No.

CLARABELLE: I wonder why he didn't meet me. Are
you his brother?

NICK: Brother?

CLARABELLE: Herman, *su hermano, su casa*
How you say, *mi casa*?
You are so handsome
Attractivo muy, mi caballero
This Claro was O K, but a bit on the rough side
don't you think?
But you, *señor*, you are a bit of alright.
we could go hide
in the blink
Of an eye, they'd never find us

haciendo dulce musica hermosa
Muy agradable, I'd be your *esposa*

NICK: Claro is gone. Claro has no brother. My name is Nick.

CLARABELLE: What a way to treat a lady?

NICK: This is Magno Rubio.

CLARABELLE: Magno—? Yes, yes. Magno, how are you?

(Here MAGNO *says something in Tagalog.)*

CLARABELLE: What's he saying?

*(*MAGNO *says something in Tagalog to* NICK.*)*

NICK: He's just very happy to see you.

CLARABELLE: Doesn't he speak, ah what? *Inglese?*
He's been writing me all these letters. You should see them, Nickie boy.
The things he says—mooey delicioso!
Are you sure you don't, how you say— *Tenga la bonedad un poco tiempo*
Take my tiempo, feel my *tiempo,* racing *mucho uno mas uno uno mas*
Never mind. I can take a well-placed hint
This is what I like to tell mi chico Magno:
He's a bit of a cutie. What a winning smile—the Pepsodent Kid!
I must check in a hotel before we talk things over. I need some expense money. And tell him I sold our engagement ring. Tell him I need another ring.

NICK: He can't do it today, Clarabelle. The banks are closed now.

*(*MAGNO *pulls money out of his wallet and hands it to* CLARABELLE.*)*

*(*CLARABELLE *takes the money.)*

CLARABELLE: *Mucho dinero*. Muchath grathiath
We'll get married *mañana*, Magno.
(She sings—)
Mañana, mañana, mañana is good enough for me

NICK: You should speak to him, be with him alone.

CLARABELLE:
I can't, Herman. I don't understand what he says.
All those g-g-g-g-gas. What IS that?

NICK: No comprendo, chica g-g-g-g-gringa.

(CLARABELLE throws MAGNO a kiss.)

CLARABELLE: Have you got a car, Magno? *El coche. El camion. Muy importante.* Never mind. How about my expense *dinero* Magno?

(MAGNO gives CLARABELLE more money.)

CLARABELLE: Bethoth y abrathoth—

(CLARABELLE kisses MAGNO on his small flat black nose.)

(The CHORUS coalesces.)

NICK: On the tip of his small flat nose
she kisses him and turns
She? Yes, she recoils
His blood simmers, boils

CLARO: On the tip of his flat black nose

he feels it itch and burn
Her eyes achingly blue
—Kiss her. It's what to do
He leans in with his killer mouth
His tongue's out, his nostrils drip

ATOY: On the pout of his lower lip
He arches north; she marches south
A moment, o so fleeting, charged with desire
   unrequited

Two souls, finally meeting,
One an angel; the other a liar

PRUDENCIO: *Diyos ko sayang na sayang* [Lord, what a pity]
love is blighted
It would take the simplest gesture now
To bring back a life forever broken

ATOY:
Just one word's too much; she doesn't know how
What could have mended is left unspoken.

(CLARABELLE *walks away.*)

NICK: 'Twas the night before Clara the Belle of us all
Ev'ry *manong* was snoring 'cept Magno the Tall

CLARO:
He was pacing and dancing and counting the hours
He'd forgotten forgotten forgotten the flowers

ATOY:
But she loved him she loved him she loved him or not
All those petals he'd pluck 'til he'd get what he got

PRUDENCIO:
He was Magno our hero so handsome and bright
If he just if he just could get through just this night

(*It's night in the bunkhouse and the croakings and heavings of the men, once again, fill the air.* MAGNO *is tossing, turning, sleepwalking, nightmareing.*)

MAGNO: Clarabella laughing smiling smiling laughing
Take my hand

(*The* CHORUS *has gathered.*)

CHORUS: Magno smiling laughing laughing smiling
such a cutie, she's your beauty
take her in marriage you'll beat the band

MAGNO:
Clarabella shining beaming, o so lovely, kiss me now

CHORUS: Hold him close and never let him breathe

MAGNO: Clarabella never let me never let me breathe

CHORUS: Magno Magno turning blue
Breathing breathing don't suit you

MAGNO: Clarabella choking, tell me you are joking
You're a fake
Let me wake
Take your hands off my throat
You're my ewe, I'm your goat
What can I do
Please love me too

CHORUS: Rosy-fingered dawn is breaking
Magno's up for air
Are there miracles a-shaking
Is fair foul, foul fair
His glass is empty, he still thinks it's full
When push comes to shove, is a pull on your pud
better than love?
Not for our little Magno for whom hope springs eternal
He thinks there's a heaven
we think it's infernal

(*Ever upbeat* MAGNO *seizes* NICK.)

MAGNO: This is the day, Nick!

NICK: Where are you going to get married?

MAGNO: New Mexico. It's the nearest place.

NICK: I'll drive you to the hotel.

MAGNO: Let me ask for her.

NICK: By all means.

(*They arrive at the hotel.*)

MAGNO: Clarabelle. Please.

CLARO: (*As a very officious clerk*) She just checked out.
Her husband came for her.

MAGNO: Her husband?

(*We see a car with* CLARABELLE *and a man with a pencil-thin moustache race by. They are smiling and laughing.*)

(MAGNO *is speechless. Then* MAGNO *finds his speech.*)

MAGNO: They are happy, Nick.

(CLARABELLE *is smiling her beautiful smile. And laughing*)

MAGNO: I'll guess we'll start picking the tomatoes next week, Nick.

NICK: Yeah.

MAGNO: Well, what are we waiting for? Let's hurry back to the bunkhouse. Those guys will eat all the chicken!

(*The* CHORUS *descends.*)

NICK: What does it profit a man if he loses the whole world, but keeps his soul

CLARO: What does it—if he never has any of the world to begin with

ATOY:
What does it—if he comes to this land and he is meek and he does not inherit the earth
for the earth is not his
no matter that his hands and feet and face and eyes
are encrusted with the earth

PRUDENCIO: What does it—that he has tilled the vineyard from the earliest morn
and his pay is seized and reduced
and only good at the company store

NICK:
What does it—that he mourns and he is not comforted

CLARO:
What does it—that he hungers and thirsts for dignity

when the signs, the "Dogs and Filipinos positively not allowed" signs do not come down

ATOY: What does it—that he is clean of heart,
he still does not see God

PRUDENCIO: What does it—that he would be a peacemaker
then keep that peace over and over again
except when he needs to lash back

NICK: What does it—that he suffers persecution for
  Justice's sake
rips the blind fold from her eyes
shouts in her ears
"See the Kingdom of Heaven; it is mine, it is ours"

ALL: Magno Rubio Filipino boy
Magno Rubio Fili—Pinoy
Magno Rubio four feet six inches tall
Magno Rubio dark as a coconut ball
With limbs like a turtle and a head real small
He hurtles over life, his spirits fly
What keeps him going, his engine non-stop
Whatever he's picking, lettuce or grapes
On hillsides, in mud, you'd think he'd just die
You'd think he'd be fed-up, bottom to top
And yet he keeps scratching just like the apes
But he's no monkey, nor a peon—No!
He's a tall man, an aristocrat—Yes!
From Luzon *pulo hilaga* Pilipinas
Though he's much on his knees, or using a hoe
He's a big man, patrician, more not less
He's our man, round and brown
like prickly juicy pinyas

NARRATOR/NICK:
Magno Rubio watched the couple pull away.
He was speechless for a moment.
Then he understood everything.

He brushed his eyes with a finger and took my arm
Later I would tell him the story of Robinson Crusoe
The world is an island, Magno
We are cast upon the sea of life
hoping to land somewhere in the world
But there is only one island—
and it is in the heart.

ATOY & CLARO: Magno Rubio

ALL: Filipino Boy

ATOY & CLARO: Magno Rubio

ALL: Fili—Pinoy
Magno Rubio four feet six inches tall
Magno Rubio dark as a coconut ball

(Tapos)

END OF PLAY

CPSIA information can be obtained
at www.ICGtesting.com
Printed in the USA
BVHW01s2152050218
506824BV00004B/86/P